Table of Contents

Introduction

Wicca is a belief system which celebrates life and nature. It focuses on the changing cycles of the year, as well as changing cycles of our own life. While our culture promotes development and progress, fast living and constantly pushes us to work more, buy more and have more, Wicca stands for a peaceful and harmonious way of life in which people make an effort to slow down and notice the world around them.

During the last 100 years, our focus on "progress" degraded the earth to such an extent, that not only have water, soil and air become toxic, but the over-exploitation of natural resources and release of vast amounts of agricultural chemicals into the environment, had resulted in a global climate change, the consequences of which we are only beginning to experience.

Wiccans believe that the Divine is present in nature, and so nature should be honored and respected. Everything from animals and plants to trees and rocks are elements of the sacred. By damaging our natural environment, we are eating away at our own life support systems.

Wicca way of life revolves around the Wheel of the Year which is marked by festivals on each solstice and equinox. These are very important times as it is believed that as seasons change, the creative power of Nature is vitalized and can be tapped for magical purposes.

Rituals are an important element of Wicca practice. They are linked to the seasons and moon phases. Moon is central in all Wicca festivals because the Wicca calendar is based on lunar year. Moon phases, and the Full Moon in particular, are seen as auspicious times when doing magic comes easy.

Many Wiccans embrace magic as part of their practice. Magic helps you get things done, on the basis on your inner power. Wicca teaches you how to plug into a wider wisdom that seems to know what's right for you and use magic to cause changes to occur in accordance with your desires.

We live in a fast-paced, hectic world where information overload, toxic environment and stressful lifestyle make us sick, frustrated and permanently exhausted. We are obsessed with being young, beautiful, successful, perfect. Instead, we are strung out, disillusioned and often angry.

In stark contrast to modern lifestyle, Wicca lifestyle is soothing and healing. Living according to its principles and embracing its uplifting, nature-focused beliefs will help you find inner peace and make sense of this hectic world of ours.

Wiccans draw strength and inspiration from the elements, the heavenly bodies and all the creatures on the earth. In a world dominated by a cult of wealth and power, Wicca can help you rediscover the spiritual connection to nature and teach you how to tune in to your inner self.

Chapter 1

What is Wicca?

Wicca is one of the Neopagan religions based on ancient, northern European Pagan beliefs and is associated with the Celts and their culture. It's believed that Wicca began in prehistory as a ritual related to the hunt and fertility themes, and over time developed into a religion of Moon-based worship.

It survived the Roman, Saxon and Norman invasions by going underground, but suffered a major loss during Christian persecution and burning of the witches, which in some countries of Western Europe lasted until the 18th century. It was revived and recreated as a religion in the 1950s by Gerald Gardner, and although it is not an ancient religion, it includes old esoteric knowledge.

Wicca, as practiced today, is a reconstruction of what little record of Celtic religious practices have remained, as well as of information on other ancient nature-based religions that pre-dated all the mainstream religions of today.

Wicca is usually associated with witchcraft, which is nothing more than a skill that many adopt as part of their spirituality. Simply put, witchcraft is the practice of various forms of magic.

The term "witch" derives its name from the ancient Anglo-Saxon word "wicca" meaning "wise".
Witchcraft in ancient history was known as "The Craft of the Wise" because most of those who followed the path were in tune with the forces of nature, had a considerable knowledge of herbs and medicines, gave council and were usually valuable parts of the community. Their role was probably similar to that of Shamans, who are respected healers and leaders in many cultures even today.

Individuals practicing witchcraft were known by many names: "wise women", "cunning men" , witches, wizards, sorcerers, etc. They were a recognized part of European rural life as late as the 19th century, and were respected as well as feared. They helped by performing magic as protection against other witchcraft, offered healing, did fortune-telling and prepared love spells and potions.

Witchcraft is an important element of Wicca practice. Despite being demonized and often represented in unflattering ways (as old, ugly, mean, evil, etc) they are ordinary group of people. Most of them have a deep regard for nature and many take active part in environmental movements.

Basically, witches are people who believe that more exists in this world and beyond than can be explained by science. And just because something cannot be proved scientifically, shouldn't mean it doesn't exist. True witches have a strong spiritual connection to the elements of the earth and they see themselves as "keepers of balance".

There are different traditions of Wicca but they all share certain core principles. These basic beliefs are:

☐ **Practice**

Being a pagan religion, Wicca is not based on doctrine, but on practice. Wicca do not have a scripture that details the religious practices or sets out "rules" one has to follow in order to belong to this movement. The Wiccan philosophy is learned through observation, participation and practice.

☐ **Divinity**

Wiccans strongly believe in balancing masculine and feminine forces, which means that both the male and female deities are honored. A Wiccan may honor a non-specific god or goddess, or they may choose to worship specific deities of their own tradition, eg Isis and Osiris, Apollo and Athena, etc.

Besides, Wiccans believe that the Divine is present in all of us. We are all sacred beings, and interaction with the gods is not limited just to the "selected few" (ie the priests or high-power individuals).

☐ **Holidays**

Holidays are based on the seasonal cycles. In Wicca, there are eight major

Sabbats (ie days of power), as well as monthly Esbats (ie lunar holy days) .

The Sabbats are the eight solar based holy days, also called the Wheel of the Year. These holy days fall on the solstices and the equinoxes and the points halfway between them.

The Esbats take place monthly on the full moon, the dark moon, and the first crescent.

☐ **Wiccan tools of trade**

Witchcraft rites require certain tools. These are the main ones:

1. Athame

This is a double sided, ritual knife used for many purposes, but never for cutting. It is either created by its owner, or is a re-worked purchased knife. This ceremonial blade usually has a black handle and represents the main ritual tool used in Wicca. In some ways, it has the same purpose as a magic wand has for fairies, ie it is primarily used to channel and direct psychic energy in Wiccan rituals and spells.

2. Altar

What an altar contains depends on your budget, a particular element you want to invoke or a spell you are trying to cast. You can set up a permanent altar, a seasonal one or an altar to celebrate a special occasion. These are some of the basic items, but you can use your imagination and create whatever feels right for you:

- A chalice or a goblet to hold a drink
- A pentacle, a five-pointed star engraved on a disk
- A cauldron, for mixing herbs and essences
- A bell which is rung at certain times during a ritual
- A bowl of water representing the element of water
- A bowl of salt representing the element of earth
- Incense representing the element of air
- Two candles, representing the God and Goddess and the element of fire

3. A wand or a sword

- This is used for casting a circle.

4. Candles

Candle color should match the energy you are trying to summon (eg red for passion, blue for calm, green for health, etc), although white ones can be used instead.

☐ **Rites of passage**

Wicca is not a formal religion and there are very few prescribed rituals and practices. Many Wiccans choose to create their own rituals for certain special occasions in their life. However, most Wiccans choose to participate in the main Wiccan rites of passage:

- <u>Dedication</u> (this is when a person confirms an interest in the craft).

- <u>Initiation</u> (a time when a person symbolically dies and is reborn as a Wiccan when a new name may be adopted).

- <u>Handfasting</u> (this was originally a marriage for a one year period. Today, most Wiccans regard it as a creating of a permanent partnership).

- <u>Parting of the Ways</u> (this is the end of a marriage).

- <u>Wiccaning</u> (a ceremony by which a baby is welcomed into Wicca, but does not obligate the child in any way).

- <u>Funeral Ceremony</u> (a requiem for a Wiccan who has died).

☐ **Magic**

Magic and spellwork is what most people associate with Wicca. Magic is used in a way that is nothing more than harnessing and redirecting of natural energy to create a change in the world around us. In Wicca, magic is just one of the skills or tools you learn over time. Most Wiccans use Wiccan tools (such as athame, crystals, candles, etc) and perform magical workings within a sacred circle

☐ **Spirit World**

Ancestors are spoken of with honor. Many Wiccans easily commune with the spirit world, and they feel that their ancestors are watching over them at all times. Just like in many religions still practiced today, Wiccans may ask their ancestors for advice or help at times of trouble.

☐ **Individual responsibility**

In Wicca, you are responsible for your own actions. This applies to both your everyday life, as well as to your work with magic. This means that you must be ready to accept both good and bad consequences of your behavior and actions, as well as those that may result from your use of magic.

    ☐   **Harm no one**

This is something most Wiccans strictly adhere to. It means that whatever magic you engage in, it must not be intentionally or even subconsciously intended to do harm to any individual.

Wiccans believe in the principle of the Three-fold Law which is one of their basic beliefs. This is a universal spiritual principle which can be summed up as: What you give out, returns to you magnified.

Chapter 2

How to become a Wiccan

There are many traditions of Wicca and for a beginner it can be very confusing and even off-putting.
Of the two core traditions (Gardnerian and Alexandrian) several other traditions arose:

–   British Traditional Wicca (Gardnerian, Alexandiran, Central Valley, Algard, Blue Star Wicca)
–   Eclectic Wicca
–   Celtic Wicca
–   Saxon Wicca
–   Dianic Wicca
–   Faiery Wicca
–   Georgian Wicca
–   Odyssean Wicca
–   Wiccan Church (New Reformed Orthodox Order of the Golden Dawn; Church and School of Wicca; Circle Sanctuary; Covenant of the Goddess; Aquarian Tabernacle Church; Rowan Tree Church; Covenant of Unitarian Universalists Pagans; Coven of the Far Flung Net).

Although they all differ, these are often just minor differences in the way a ritual is performed, Sabbats are observed, etc.

However, if you are contemplating joining Wicca, it's best to ignore all these traditions (at least for the time being) and focus on core Wicca values. Only that way will you know if Wicca is right for you or not.

Here are some guidelines to help you make the decision:

☐ Try to find out as much as you can about Wicca, so as to fully understand what you can expect of this movement and what may be expected of you, once you join. Read everything you can find on Wicca or witchcraft, join Forums and read on-line Wicca magazines. Follow discussions among Wiccans and study the questions some would-be Wiccans have. Do as much research as you can so as to first of all fully understand what Wicca is and what it isn't.

☐ Wicca doesn't have strict rules and regulations, however, there is one basic principle that you have to be very clear about:

Do no harm

If you plan on joining Wicca to learn how to do spells and perform magic to get back at someone, or to steal someone's husband or a job, then think again. Spells done to harm others, will eventually come back to you.

Personal energy is a powerful tool which is why you should use it consciously. If you put out a spell to take revenge upon someone, the negative energy you invest in such a spell will, sooner or later, come right back at you. The same goes for positive energy, so remember, kindness pays.

☐ Many Wiccans join a coven (a group of Wiccans), but just as many do solitary Wicca and perform rituals and spells on their own. If you are going solitary, start small. Try to learn about rituals and spells and start by doing simple ones, until you learn how to cast a circle, perform magic, do visualization, etc.

☐ Create an altar. There is no need to spend vast amounts of money on this. You can create a beautiful altar with things you already have at home. What's important is to do it meaningfully. An altar needs to be clean and contain items that have your personal touch.

You can start by having a candle (you can buy different color candles later, for spells requiring different types of energy (eg red for passion, yellow for energy, etc) and objects representing the four elements (air, water, fire, earth).

Items that can represent the four elements are:

<u>Air</u>: feathers, images or figurines of birds, etc.
<u>Fire</u>: candles, incense, red glassware, red or orange items
<u>Water</u>: bowl of water, blue items, sea shells, coral
<u>Earth</u>: crystals, stones, brown or yellow items, terracotta items

☐   Start celebrating Sabbats. These are times of the year which mark the changing of the seasons. There are 8 Sabbats and you may choose to celebrate all or just some of them. You can make elaborate preparations for Sabbats, or you can simply light a candle (or a fire if you have a garden), leave some offerings for Mother Earth (eg bird feed, or some food for any stray or wild animal that will find it) and say a prayer for yourself or someone else. By celebrating the seasons you are honoring Mother Earth.

☐   Understand that the Divine is all around you. Everything is sacred. Everyone is sacred. Respect that. Don't ever do something that could destroy the environment of someone's life.

☐   Learn to listen to your intuition, as this is often the best guidance you will get, especially in times of trouble. We usually ignore that little voice that often acts as our conscious or the sixth sense. It's amazing how often we come up with excuses for ignoring what our sub-conscious is telling us, rather than face the truth or make some tough decisions.

☐   Accept responsibility for your words, actions, thoughts as well as for the consequences of your magical works. Having the power to change reality (yours and other peoples') is a huge responsibility. Don't only take advantage of your skills, take the responsibility for them as well.

In Wicca, the world is metaphysically viewed in terms of four elements -.earth, water, air and fire. Each of the elements represents a certain quality, and ideally, all four elements should be equally represented both in magic and in our own lives:

- Earth is solid and grounding
- Water is emotion and wisdom
- Air stands for intellect and creativity
- Fire is the element of strength and a symbol of life

The reason elements are invoked during spell casting is that the core energy of each of the elements needs to be raised and be present throughout the ritual.

By casting a circle you prepare an area as a ritual space. The cardinal points (north, south, east and west) are usually marked with something that represents an element. The traditional system puts earth in the north, air in the east, fire in the south and water in the west. So, when casting a circle you mark the north with something that represents earth, in the west you put something that stands for water, etc. That way, the space within these elements, which is where you stand, becomes a sacred space where spells can be cast.

Although Pagans always performed their rituals outside, because Nature was their temple, and many Wiccans still do, for practical reasons, rituals often have to be performed indoors. This is partly because of the weather (it could be snowing or pouring with rain), and partly for security reason, since many rituals need to be performed at night, during certain Moon phases.

During spellwork, you are expected to ask for a presence of a certain Goddess and God, those who represent a particular element. There are quite a few names you could draw on, so find out beforehand which deities you are going to call upon, and remember that Wicca believes in polarity of the Divine and thus one always invokes both the Goddess and the God.

Besides, each of the elements has its own elemental. Elementals are nature spirits that you can summon during spell work and ask for their help. Once you have the help of an elemental, casting spells become easy. You only have to hold it (in your mind) and request its help.

Also, to successfully represent elements, it's best to use colors typical of each element (eg brown for earth, red for fire, etc).

Earth

Earth element is represented in the North quarter of the circle and items placed there should be symbolic of earth, eg crystal, dish of earth, a piece of wood, etc. The primary earth Goddess is Mother Nature or Gaia.

You can use Earth in rituals to bring stability and security. You can also do earth spells for fertility, growth, family matters, healing, material issues, practical matters as well as bringing things/projects to fruition.

If you are doing a spell for any of these issues and want to decorate your home altar with earth elements, you can use crystals, the pentacle, stones, pieces of wood, soil, food, flowers, herbs.

The elemental spirits of earth are tree-spirits, trolls and fairies. Earth colors are brown, black, green and gold so keep this in mind when decorating your altar.

<u>Preparation for spellwork</u>

Prepare your sacred space by clearing away the clutter, then do some self-cleansing to calm your mind and open your chakras. This can be achieved by sitting quietly while you relax and try to free your mind of inner chatter. Make sure to switch off your phone and take pets out of the room!

Find something that represents earth and is pointed. This will work as an extension of your aura (eg twig, wooden spoon, a bone, a crystal). Holding it in your hand, imagine an earth barrier forming around you (eg a wall of trees, a shield of leaves, etc). Stand still and feel the energy flowing through your body. Ask for the presence of the Goddess as Gaia and the God as the Green Man. Sit inside the circle and meditate on the earth. Think about how you want to help yourself or others.

For the spell to work, you now need to raise your power and you can do this by using a rattle, drum, dance, shaking your body, clapping your hands, etc. You may also chant. At the end of the ritual, ground yourself by shaking your hands and stamping your feet.

Consecrate some earthy food and drink with the element of earth, asking the Gods to bless your ritual (eg baked potatoes or some bread) and take these gifts to the earth and be grateful (ie when you finish with spellwork take the food offering outside and leave it for birds or stray or wild animals to take).

Give thanks to the Goddess and God for helping you, then close the circle in reverse order.

The best way to meet earth elementals is to go outside. Nature is everywhere and the spirits of earth inhabit all places. Find a spot, or a tree, or a lake, that "speaks" to you and visit it as often as you can.

Air

Air element is represented in the East quarter of the circle, and can be symbolized by feathers, smudge and incense, bells, wind chimes, carved birds, scented herbs, songs. Air colors are pale gray, white, blue and yellow.

The element of air is also known as an element of purification and transformation. As a source of light it is protective, but it can also be chaotic and destructive.

Air is the element of intellect, study, youth, creativity, communication and travel and can be used for spells concerning any of these issues.

If you want to cast spells invoking the element of air, you first have to cleanse yourself with air and you can do this using a smudge bundle made of sage or an incense stick. Waft the scent all over you and symbolically clean your aura. While breathing in the scent, you are clearing your mind from negative thoughts. Or, if you have time, you can go for a brief walk and thus relieve your body of stress.

Air magic can help with spells for birth, beginnings, new initiatives, inviting circumstances into your life, healing of the mind, children, exams and interviews, communication and legal matters.

Cast the circle as described for Earth, but use items representing Air and place them in the East.

If you want to ask Air elementals to help you with your spellwork, invoke sylphs or fairies of trees, flowers and winds.

Ask for the presence of Goddess Aradia and God Enlil.

Fire

The fire element is situated in the South of the circle. Fire represents our energy, both creative and destructive, and also stands for passion, anger and love. The Wiccan tools of fire are candles, lamps, the athame, amber and other red/orange crystals. Colors are orange, red, gold, yellow.

Fire represents action and life. It is the element of strength, both physical and mental.

You can use fire in magic to deal with anger but also to attract happiness and money, to get rid of things, to bring creative energy, etc. Fire spells are related to love, happiness, anger, money and desire.

Destructive force of fire can be used in rituals if we want to get rid of things. Write down what (or who) you want to get rid of, and burn the paper in a flame, stating that as the paper burns it destroys the thing (or person) you want to get rid of.

You can also use fire magic to bring love into your life. But remember, to bring love you need to love yourself. Light a red candle and as it burns ask fire to help you love yourself. While the candle burns, love yourself.

We can only truly connect with fire elementals (salamanders) when live fire is present. However, as this is usually not possible, we have to use a candle instead. Night is the best time to meet with nature spirits of fire, as they are more visible at this time.

Cast the circle as described for Earth, but use items that represent Fire and place them in the South.

If you want to ask Fire elementals to help you with your spellwork, invoke salamanders.

Ask for the presence of Goddess Brighid and God Agni.

The Water element

Water element is normally represented in the West quarter of the circle, relating to autumn and twilight. Items to represent water in the circle or on you altar are water itself, the chalice or cup, the scrying bowl, and mirrors.

Water is seen as the element of the emotions and balance, and water magic is needed to bring balance to our emotions. It is associated with the moon (the tides). Water colors are all shades of blue, white and sometimes gray or green. Water magic is needed to bring balance to our emotions.

Water also stands for wisdom and is the element of intuition and divination. It can represent death and rebirth, just as baptism is a symbolic death and rebirth.

Cast the circle as described for Earth, but use items representing Water element and place them in the West.

If you want to ask Water elemental spirits to help you with your spellwork, invoke nymphs, mermaids or fairies of ponds, lakes and streams.

Ask for the presence of Goddess Diana and God Neptune.

Seasonal celebrations

Our ancestors lived according to the rhythms of nature and their festivals celebrated these rhythms. To stress the human relationship with the Earth's seasons, they marked particular points in the year with celebrations which usually began at sundown the day before, and ended on the following sundown.

There were 8 of these festivals (or Sabbats) which were celebrated to mark the beginning of a particular season, and they made up the Wheel of the Year. By celebrating the cycle of birth, life, death and rebirth our pagan ancestors stayed in close touch with Nature and maintained a spiritual connection to the earth.

The eight Sabbats are: Samhain, Yule, Imbolc, Ostara, Beltain, Litha, Lughnasadh and Mabon.

There were also the Esbats, festivals which were celebrated on the 13 full moons that occur every year. These festivals celebrated the Goddess at her height of power, as Pagans believed that the Full Moon was the time when the Goddess magic was stronger than at any other day of the month.

Many of these festivals were marked by nature's changes rather than by the calendar, but today, they are all calendar-based:

Ostara (Spring equinox): 21/22 March
Litha (Summer solstice): 21/22 June
Modron (Autumn equinox): 21/22 September
Yule (Winter solstice): 21/22 December

Imbolc: 1/2 February
Beltane: 1 May
Lammas: 1/2 August
Samhain: 31 October

Basically, Wiccans have a major festival roughly every six weeks. Of these, four mark the agricultural year and occur on the solstices and equinoxes, while the other four occur on the days that fall exactly between each major Sabbat – in May, August, October and February.

In the past, ritual battles between light and dark, good and evil or life and death were fought during the seasonal festivals. This was usually a period of three days that marked the change of one seasonal tide to the next, and by celebrating the Sabbats, our ancestors aligned themselves with the cosmic wisdom.

Sabbats

Summer Solstice (21/22 June)

This festival marks the longest day of the year and is also known as Midsummer.

This is the time to gather strength from the Sun before the day starts shortening. *Litha* is supposed to mean "wheel", representing the sun. During the ceremony, bonfires are lit and people leap over the fire for purification and renewed energy. Traditionally, vigil is kept on the night of the 20th June, to witness the rising sun on the longest day of the year, 21st June.

Summer solstice is believed to be a particularly auspicious time for renewal and enhancement of health, finances, joy, faith, love, friendship, abundance. Midsummer festival celebrates the Sun at its strongest and rituals performed on this occasion emphasize the power, the abundance and the magic of Summer.

The main element of the *Litha* ritual is fire (representing the Sun), while passion and excitement drive the festival.

Winter Solstice (20/21 December)

This marks the shortest day of the year.

The focus of this Sabbat is the return of the Sun's reign over the sky, as from here on the days will once again become longer than the nights.

While the return of the light is barely perceptible, honoring its presence gives us strength to endure what remains of winter. It's like seeing the light at the end of the tunnel.

In many pagan traditions and cultures the idea of eternal return is expressed through the ritual use of trees, so the Yule log burns for the entire festival.

As far as spellwork is concerned, winter is a powerful time for banishing, grounding, meditation, inner work and spells related to dormancy, endings, silence. Winter solstice is believed to be an auspicious time to find answers within.

Long, dark nights are a good opportunity to do some inner work, contemplate and reflect on the year behind you, while preparing yourself for the creative and life-giving energy of the spring.

Spring Equinox (21/22 March)

This marks the time when hours of light and darkness are equal.

On this day, Wiccans and many other Neopagans celebrate the arrival of Spring and the earth's awakening from a long, harsh winter. The key focus of this Sabbat is rebirth.

This Sabbat is also celebrated as the day of equilibrium (equal hours of light and darkness) and transition (of winter to summer) and is a good time to perform self-banishings and do spellwork to gain things you have lost, or qualities you wish you had.

Autumn Equinox (21/22 September)

This marks the time when hours of light and darkness are equal.

On this Sabbat we celebrate the second of three harvest festivals as well as yet another change of seasons. We give thanks for the warm days of plenty which are behind us, as we prepare for the cold and dark days of winter that lie ahead.

This Sabbat is a kind of thanks-giving. Crops have been collected and stored for the coming winter and we can relax and enjoy the fruits of our work.

Mabon is the time of giving thanks for the things we have, be it abundant crops or other blessings.

Samhain: 31 October

Samhain means "first frost". Many Wiccans consider it the main Pagan festival as it marks not only the beginning of winter, but the beginning of a Pagan New Year. To Celts, this was a key point of the year's turning, a chance to begin anew.

Winter is a time for turning inwards. The dropping temperatures encourage us to stay indoors, rest and nurture ourselves in preparation for the warmth of spring. This is a good time to reflect and contemplate and receive messages from "within" (ie from the unconscious).

Samhain is also the time to remember the dead. This is believed to be a magical time when the veil between the world of the dead and the living is thin and when contacting the dead is easy. In rituals performed at this time one must honor, remember and speak of the dead.

Like all other Sabbats, Samhain is a time of transition. As we prepare to move from hot dry summer to cold wet winter, we celebrate the never-ending cycle of life, death and rebirth.

Imbolc means "ewe's milk". This is the time when the first snow drops and crocus appear, as well as the first lambs. The Imbolc festival has strong association with the Celtic fire goddess Brigid, with fire symbolising the strengthening of the Sun.

The focus of this Sabbat is on the first signs of Spring. This is when we celebrate the rebirth of the Sun and the new cycle of growth.

Imbolc being a half way point between winter and spring, is considered an auspicious time for initiation into Wicca covens.

Beltane: 1 May

Also known as May day, Festival of fire, Witches night.

The focus of this Sabbat is on the fertility of Nature and the greening of the Earth. During the celebrations, rituals are performed to welcome the Green Man, or spirit of Nature.

Beltane is the time of natural magic, when Wiccans make offerings to the spirits of Nature and the elements. On this day, we witness the union of the God and the Goddess in the sacred marriage, the result of which is new life and fertility of all living things. This union is symbolized by the dance around the Maypole.

The highlight of this day is giving thanks for the new life that's on its way.

Lammas, also called *Lughnasadh*, was the celebration of the annual wheat harvest. This was the first harvest festival of the year and because a good harvest meant a difference between life and death, during this Sabbat people prayed and offered sacrifices for the success of future crops.

Today, when food is available throughout the year, and majority of people live in cities, this Sabbat is perhaps not as important as it used to be. However, Wiccans celebrate this day not just to give thanks for the crops but to mark the change of seasons. The Sun God symbolically loses some of his strength and as each night grows longer, we start preparations for the short cold days of winter.

Ancient ceremonies originating in the belief that there is a spiritual essence embodied in plants, animals, mountains, lakes, etc are still celebrated today not only in Wicca, but slightly disguised as Christian celebrations of Christmas, Easter, Halloween, All Souls Day, etc.

Trees, and especially the oak, played a big part in Pagan worship. For the ancients, the annual death and rebirth of nature was a great mystery drama, whose meaning was celebrated in their myths and rituals.

Witnessing all vegetation dying and receding to the dark womb of Mother Earth in Winter, and coming back to life with the first signs of Spring, in the eyes of our ancestors, was nothing but a miracle.

The Wicca Sabbats are celebrations of the miracle of Life.

Chapter 5

The Power of the Moon

Wiccans revere the Moon as the primary Pagan Goddess. Through her various phases, the Moon affects and controls all life on earth, eg it causes the tides by the gravitational pull on the waters of the ocean, and in turn, tides affect fishing, weather, rivers, etc.

Besides, the Full Moon has a particularly powerful effect on humans. It's well-known that there are more instances of crime, violence and irrational behavior when the Moon is full and that many psychiatric patients become more disturbed and agitated during this period.

The Moon was very important for the ancients, helping them to measure time and to determine when the best time was for planting and harvesting crops. It also helped mariners the seas.

Moon deities

The moon is associated with the divine feminine and as the feminine cycles are linked to the phases of the Moon, it's not surprising that most lunar deities were female.

The Moon Goddess was an important deity in many cultures and religions and some of the best known names of the Goddess are:

- ☐   **Andromeda** (Greek) - Although today she is linked with the stars many scholars believe that Andromeda was a pre-Hellenic moon deity.

- ☐   **Anunit** (Babylonian) - Goddess of the moon and battle. She was also associated with the evening star and later became known as Ishtar.

- ☐   **Arianrhod** (Celtic) – Goddess of hte Moon and stars, her name means "silver wheel" ie the wheel of the year and the web of fate.

- ☐   **Artemis** (Greek) - The Greek Goddess of the hunt, nature and birth. This maiden Goddess is symbolized by the crescent moon.

- ☐   **Cerridwen** (Celtic) - This crone, Goddess is most famous for her cauldron of wisdom. She was the mother of the great bard Taliesin, and is deeply linked to the image of the waning moon.

One of the most powerful Moon rituals performed in Wiccan rites is *Drawing Down the Moon*. The ritual usually takes place on the night of the Full Moon when the practitioner calls to the Goddess to enter her and speak through her.

Although this ritual often requires entering into a trance-like state, and many a coven's High Priestess will do just that, a solitary practitioner can, with some practice, learn how to perform this ritual.

If your mind is free of chatter and you manage to tune into cosmic wisdom, after a while, you will start feeling a kind of energy entering your body. The very sensitive people who easily pick-up vibes from their environment, may even feel a heightened sense of clairty over the next few days.

Moon phases

Wiccans take into account the Moon phase whenever planning magic work, because each phase of the Moon has its own energy. When spell-casting, the more you can align with the flow of Universal Energy, the more powerful your spells will be.

The phases of the Moon are:

☐   Dark Moon: This is a time when the Moon is not visible in the sky and this phase lasts for approximately three days.
☐   New Moon: Silver crescent which rises in the West (in the Northern Hemisphere).
☐   Waxing Moon: This is a period when the Moon grows.
☐   Full Moon: The Moon at its full glory, rising in the East (in the Northern Hemisphere).
☐   Waning Moon: This is when the size of the Moon starts receding.

Wiccans know that the Moon carries different energies as it sails through the sky, so for purposes of spellwork, and based on the Moon's vibrancy in a particular month, the Moon is given a different name for every month of the year:

January

The January Moon is known as the Wolf Moon. This is a good time to do some inner work in preparation for the New Year and new beginning. Use this moon to perform self-cleansing rituals and make plans for the year ahead.

February

The name for the February Moon is the Ice Moon.

During this month we begin to feel the strength of female energy. Deep under the snow, new life stirs and the first crocus or snowdrops appear. Time to start preparing for new beginning.

March

This Moon is referred to as the Storm Moon. Amidst rains and storms, the energy of life swarms the earth. Feel the power of nature and let your imagination and creativity be inspired.

April

The name of this Moon is the Growing Moon. Everything around you is growing as the world of Nature is being renewed. During this time you can focus on personal growth and start new projects.

May

The name for this Moon is the Hare Moon. During this month we celebrate the sexual energy of nature and new life we are blessed with.

June

The Moon name for this month is the Mead Moon, and it marks the halfway point of the year.

This is a time to take stock on what we have accomplished so far and what still needs to be done to. If you're not doing well, evaluate what has gone wrong, and what can be done about it. This is auspicious time to work magic for success at work, for improved health, or home protection.

July

The Moon of July is called the Hay Moon. The earth is ful of ripening crops and lush vegetation. There's a lot of powerful Sun energy around. Keep on doing what you're good at and find your inner reserves of strength to finish the work that you started. The abundant energy of this moon will help you.

August

This Moon is called the Corn Moon and we now celebrate our first harvest festival. In other words, if you've done everythng properly, you should start seeing the results of your hard work. Don't forget to thank those who helped you get there.

September

This Moon is called the Harvest Moon. Time to complete what you have started and tie up loose ends. The last crops have been gathered and stored for the winter. The harvest is in full swing, with abundance all around. Be thankful for what you have, even if it's less than you think you deserve. Maybe it's time to re-evaluate your efforts and change direction. This is also the time to celebrate family, friends and all those who have supported you through the year.

October

The name for this Moon is the Blood Moon. The name comes from the custom of killing and salting down livestock for the upcoming winter months, not from sacrifice as some think The nights are crisp and clear, and you can sense a change in the energy around you. Winter is approaching fast and now is a good time to plan and stock up for the months ahead.

This is the month of Samhain so use the Lunar energy to honor your ancestors and fix any family problems you might be having.

November

This Moon is called the Snow Moon. Reflect on your life and be brutally honest with yourself. Make a list of what has worked and what hasn't, learn from your mistakes, then move on.

This is not a time to start new projects, but rather to reflect and recharge your batteries.

December

The Moon for the month of December is called the Cold Moon. Over time, many of us accumulate a lot clutter, that we often find ourselves stuck without realizing what it is that's holding us back. Get rid of all excess baggage you've been carrying around, eg relationships that no longer serve any purpose, things you have been accumulating for who knows how long, behavior-patterns you've outgrown, etc. Free yourself from mental and physical clutter and start the New Year free from things, or people, holding you down.

Moon magic

Those who want to do Moon magic, have to know which Moon phases are best for what kind of spellwork. This doesn't mean you can't perform magic on any other day, however, different phases of the Moon carry different energies, and as it is these energies we are working with during spellwork, we should try and work <u>with</u> them, rather than <u>against</u> them.

For example, a spell for starting a new job or relationship, should not be done during the Waning Moon, when the energy is diminishing. On the other hand, a spell for ending an unhappy relationship would be perfect for the weeks of the Waning Moon.

There are many Moon rituals one can do, some pretty complicating, others simple and easy to do even for beginners. But, for a spell to work, the most important thing is that you are really tuned-in. Your spell should consist of words or actions which make sense to you, rather than you just repeating words and performing something someone else came up with, which you don't understand and have no idea why you are doing it. Magic spells have to make sense to YOU.

For all spellwork, and particularly for Moon magic, you should use your creativity and follow your instinct. You can put up a fancy altar or you can simply light a candle. You can wear priestess-type clothes or use special Wicca accessories, but this is not what will make your spell work.

While accessories like special types of candles, jewelry or decorations will certainly help you tune into the "Moon magic" mood, you can perform these rituals just as successfully without them.

The main thing is to mentally prepare for the spellwork by knowing what you want to achieve and aligning the spell with the phases of the Moon. Mental preparation means being clear-headed and focused on what you are about to do.

Couple of hours before the spellwork, try not to engage in any communication, switch off your phone, don't watch TV, don't read the newspapers. We live with so much information overload, and our brain processes all that information in a way which is still not fully understood, so you don't want your subconscious to be going over an SMS you had just received, or mulling over the potential effects of climate change on the world economy.

Switch off from the mundane world, relax and focus on what you are about to do.

Here are some ideas how you can use different Moon phases for magic:

Dark Moon

If you feel there is something in your life that is unnecessary (eg a bad habit or a draining relationship), now is the time to get rid of it.

The Dark Moon days are also a good time for summing-up: reflect on what you have accomplished in the previous month (or months), and plan for what you want to achieve in the future. The Dark Moon days are not considered a good time for magic, although some say that it was on these days that our ancestors carried out hexes and curses.

It's best to rest and relax during these three days, and prepare for the promise and energy that the following Moon phase brings.

New Moon

A good time for spellwork, as this phase is suitable for new projects, new beginnings and increase. New Moon is also a powerful time to work on self-healing. The focus of spellwork during this phase should be on fresh starts, optimism and hope.

Waxing Moon

As the Moon grows, so does its power. This is a good time for love, prosperity and healing energy work. During this phase, you can cast spells to increase, attract, accomplish, create, or grow something. Days of the Waxing Moon are considered auspicious time for starting a positive transformation, regardless of what it is you want to transform.

Fool Moon

You can do any kind of magic on the Full Moon, as She is at her most powerful at this time.

Traditionally, the Full Moon was most often associated with witchcraft, possibly because the very powerful Lunar energy enhances one's intuition and wisdom.

The heightened psychic awareness one can achieve during the Full Moon days helps with realization of ideas, dreams, commitments, projects.

Waning Moon

As the Moon grows smaller, her energy becomes suitable for sending things away from you: end a toxic relationship, get rid of a debt, dispel negativity, etc. Auspicious time for letting go, releasing, sand making space for new things (or people) in your life.

Blue Moon

When the Full Moon occurs twice in one month, the second full moon is a blue moon. This is an excellent time to set new goals for yourself; it is said that whatever you wish for at this time will come true. But, remember the old saying: Be careful what you wish for – you may just get it!

Lunar Eclipse

A lunar eclipse takes place on average every six months. In the past, people often thought this phenomenon to be a sign of an impending disaster, but today, a lunar eclipse is seen more as an opportunity to stop and look inwards.

A lunar eclipse occurs at the time of the Full Moon when the Sun and Moon are in opposition to one another. This creates a considerable stress and could represent the culmination of events or the end of something. Lunar eclipse often influence the relationships because of the polarity of the Sun and the

Moon, but it doesn't affect everyone every time it happens.

During a lunar eclipse we usually have to let something go (relationship, behavior, job).

As far as spellwork is concerned, the Lunar eclipse represents the union of both male and female energies (Sun – male, Moon – female) and any type of magic worked during a lunar eclipse will be greatly amplified.

Chapter 6

Practical Wicca

Those interested in Wicca can either join a coven or go solo. Many, perhaps most, Wiccans are solitary practitioners and perform their rites alone. The following text is aimed primarily at those who do not belong to covens but practice on their own and therefore the suggestions for rituals will assume there is only one person participating.

For cultures which follow Earth tradition, a year consists of two parts:

<u>Waxing Year</u> which begins at Winter Solstice and lasts until the Summer Solstice (21 December – 21 June). This period is a great time for spellwork to attract, improve, increase and strengthen.

<u>Waning Year</u> which begins at Summer Solstice (when the Sun "dies") and lasts until the Winter Solstice (when it is "reborn") ie 21 June – 21 December). This is a good time for spellwork to avert, banish, decrease, end, lessen and weaken.

The rituals and spells work best if they match energies of a particular time of the year, or the Moon phase. So, spells to attract love, improve relationships, increase income, boost one's career, etc are best performed during the waxing half of the year.

On the other hand, spells to avert bad luck, end illness, get rid of bad habits, dispel loneliness, lessen financial problems, banish negativity, etc for the maximum effect, should be performed during the waning half of the year.

Sabbats

The periods of the eight Sabbats mark the time of powerful energy shifts and participating in rituals at these times is to become saturated with the energies associated with the season.

One of the purposes of the seasonal rituals is to to harmonize us with the rhythms of Nature. Rituals are both a means of worship and a method of communicating with the deities or spirits of Nature. It is a symbolic language that allows us to, temporarily, step out of our mundane world and touch the Unknown.

It doesn't matter whether you choose to mark the Sabbats with simple or highly ritualized ceremonies. The point is to strive towards attunement with the Spirit of Nature.

The following are suggestions how to celebrate some of the Sabbats and you can use your creativity and imagination to come up with ideas for personalized rituals for major or periodic celebrations.

Samhain rituals

According to the Celtic calendar, November is the first lunar month and belongs to the birch tree, the tree of beginnings. Samhain is celebrated on the 31st of October and marks the beginning of the Celtic New Year.

This Sabbat represents the festival of the dead, the end of the harvest and the start of the coldest part of the year. The reason Samhain is associated with the dead is probably because it reflects Nature's rhythms. This time of the year marks the end of the growing season, and all the plants die. The ancients believed that the world of the living and the dead merge at this time and that it's easy to contact your ancestors during this Sabbat. For those who have lost a loved one during the past year, now is a good time to bring closure to grieving.

How to celebrate:

Samhain can be celebrated in a number of ways, but the focus always has to remain on remembering the dead and planning for the future.

- ☐ You can celebrate by putting up an altar, writing down your goals for the coming year and decorating the altar with things that represent your goals.

Decorations are whatever is available in nature at this time, which is why the typical decorations for a Samhain altar are apples, gourds, fallen leaves, straw, cornstalks, acorns, etc.

☐ You cam perform a Wicca ritual by casting a circle and marking the four cardinal directions with items representing the elements typical of that directions: North with elements of earth, East with elements of Air, South with elements of Fire and West with elements of Water.

Greet the four cardinal directions – North, East, South, and West. Greet the above and the below.

Say a prayer for the dead, remember them and thank them.

☐ Or, you can simply decorate your home (or room) with Samhain seasonal symbols and light a candle. Say a prayer for the dead.

☐ Or you could make an ancestors altar by gathering photographs of deceased family and friends, arranging them on a table or altar, lighting a few candles while you say a prayer in their honor.

☐ Or, you can visit the grave of a loved one that had passed away during the previous year. Place an offering of fresh flowers and light a candle.

Yule rituals

Winter Solstice has been celebrated for thousands of years all over the world, although under different names. The focus of this Sabbat is celebration of Light, ie the rebirth of the Sun.

In the past, Yule celebrations often lasted several days. Today, Wiccans celebrate this Sabbat by rituals, feasts, merry making.

<u>How to celebrate:</u>

☐ Decorate your home with sacred plants (holly, ivy, evergreen boughs, and pine cones) and typical Yule colors (red, green and white - or gold). Wear red or green. You may hang a sprig of mistletoe above a major

threshold and leave it there until next Yule as a good luck charm.
Decorate the Christmas (ie Solstice) Tree with Pagan symbols.

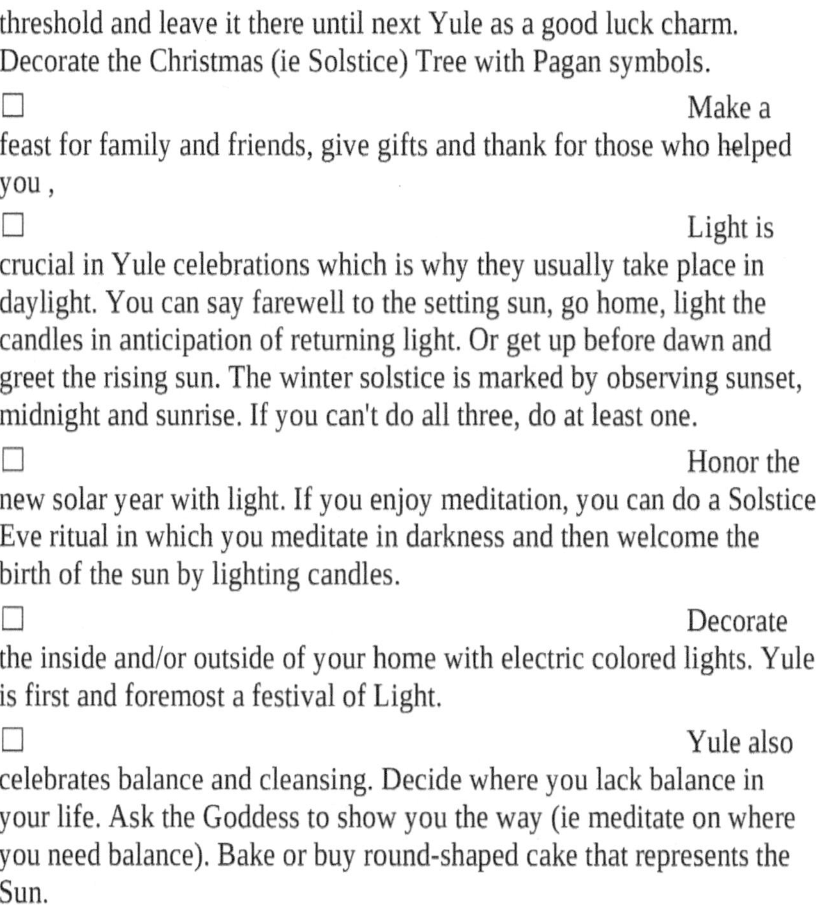

☐ Make a
feast for family and friends, give gifts and thank for those who helped
you ,

☐ Light is
crucial in Yule celebrations which is why they usually take place in
daylight. You can say farewell to the setting sun, go home, light the
candles in anticipation of returning light. Or get up before dawn and
greet the rising sun. The winter solstice is marked by observing sunset,
midnight and sunrise. If you can't do all three, do at least one.

☐ Honor the
new solar year with light. If you enjoy meditation, you can do a Solstice
Eve ritual in which you meditate in darkness and then welcome the
birth of the sun by lighting candles.

☐ Decorate
the inside and/or outside of your home with electric colored lights. Yule
is first and foremost a festival of Light.

☐ Yule also
celebrates balance and cleansing. Decide where you lack balance in
your life. Ask the Goddess to show you the way (ie meditate on where
you need balance). Bake or buy round-shaped cake that represents the
Sun.

Ostara rituals

There are many different ways you can celebrate Ostara, but it is observed by
marking the coming of Spring and the fertility of the land. If you lack ideas
for this Sabbat celebration, just pay attention to Nature and notice the
seasonal changes - the ground is becoming warmer, first plants come from
the ground, the land is becoming green again.

This festival is about new growth and green is considered a sacred color for
tis festival because it represents the greening of the land.

<u>How to celebrate</u>

    ☐   Set up an Ostara altar. Decorate it with flowers, colored eggs, potted plant, green candles, incense, etc. Stand before the altar, meditate for a few moments then say a prayer and give thanks.

    ☐   If you decide to cast a circle, decorate it with flowers. You can wear buds and blossoms in your hair.

    ☐   Or you can simply decorate your home with spring flowers, prepare Easter eggs, wear green, plant some seeds in your garden.

    ☐   Make a growth charm and decorate it with growth symbols.

Periodic rituals

There are many reasons to celebrate and do rituals and these don't have to be linked to Sabbats. Many Wiccans meet and celebrate every Full Moon. The rituals can include casting a circle and performing lengthy and complex preparations, or can consist of a prayer, lighting a candle and perhaps some ritual food (cake, wine, juice, etc)

<u>Creating a ritual</u>

Until you learn the Craft, it's best to join a coven, but you can also perform rituals on your own. With practice you will come up with ways of doing different rituals both outdoors or indoors.

These are some of the things to keep in mind when preparing for a ritual:

    ☐   Select a theme to run throughout the ritual (eg beginning of something, ending something, remembering ancestors, thanking for the harvest, etc). Decide what the ritual is for and if possible align it with the suitable Moon phase.

    ☐   Make a list of goals. Before you start a ritual make sure you know what you are doing it for. Prepare the prayers or invocations beforehand.

    ☐   Set up the altar at least couple of hours before the ritual. The process of setting it up will help you tune in and mentally prepare for the ritual you are about to perform. Altars should be set up with the purpose of the ritual in mind. Use colors, items and decorations which match the energy you are about to work with.

☐	Cleanse yourself and your sacred space.

☐	Rituals are often about balance and support. Decide where do you need balance/support in your life.

☐	Cast a circle and invoke the elements.

☐	Finish any ritual or spell working with a grounding exercise. Have a drink of water.

☐	You may wish to consecrate the food and drink you have prepared for the ritual and offer some to the earth as a token of thanks.

☐	Close by giving thanks.

Remember that ritual is a direct expression of intention. Powerful ritual is all about connecting to your own source of spirituality, which is why a self-created rituals are the most powerful. The magic works best if it resonates with you. Whenever possible, perform your rituals on the Full Moon.

Closing Chapter

This was an overview of Wicca. If what you've read resonates with you, you can easily find additional information or a coven to join.

For those who decide to delve deeper and include animal guides, astral travel, crystal magic or different kinds of divination into their Wicca practice, there is a lot of information and groups that can help them.

Wicca is a deep spiritual practice which can uplift and inspire you to live in harmony with your environment and develop a deep appreciation and awe for Nature. It also offers a gentle way to heal on every level.

When you learn to invoke divine forces or nature spirits in rituals, a whole new world will open up to you. By engaging in rituals, regular or periodic, you'll be synchronizing your lifestyle to that of Mother Nature. Rituals are a way to purify and align.

Which Wicca tradition you'll decide to follow will depend on both what's available locally and what appeals to you. However, before choosing a tradition, make sure you understand what Wicca religion is all about. Differences between different traditions are often subtle, eg: how much emphasis is placed on the spiritual, ceremonial of magical aspects; whether a tradition is more ceremonial or folk based; how is tradition passed down to subsequent generations; how much secrecy are members expected to maintain, etc.

Those serious about Wicca, will try to incorporate Wicca beliefs into their lifestyle.

In ancient cultures, and in modern-day Wicca, time was circular rather than linear. This is reflected in their commencing each day, and each festival, at dusk rather than dawn. Can you do this?

As Wicca is predominantly a Moon-based religion you should try and align your activities both ritual and mundane to lunar energies. For example, if possible, plan a trip or a new project to coincide with the New Moon, time important meetings, celebrations or dates for the Full Moon days, break up with your boyfriend during the Waning Moon days, etc.

According to Wicca, certain times of the year, particularly Samhain and Beltane, being the time between the seasons, are believed to be particularly suitable for magic, and one's perception of reality increases. For the experienced witches, November is THE time to see the past and gaze into the future, and retrieve unwritten wisdom of ancient ways.

Whether you want to practice witchcraft or not, try living your life attuned with the wisdom of Mother Earth and aligned with the vibrations of the Universe.

I want to thank you from the bottom of my heart for taking the time to read this book! I hope that this book has brought you much understanding and has provided some value to you.. If you enjoyed this book please leave a 5-star review on amazon telling me what you liked best about it. Thanks so much, and have a great day!